The New Buddhism

A Path To Nirvana

Chundi / Vajradharma

Copyright © 2013 by Vajradharma

All rights reserved under the Pan-American and International Copyright Conventions. This book may not be reproduced, in whole or in part, in any form or by any means electronic or mechanical, including photocopying, recording, or by any information storage and retrieval system now known or hereafter invented, without written permission from the publisher, and the author.

ISBN-13:
978-0615859705

ISBN-10:
0615859704

Buddhas on the Cover
(The Seven Protector Buddhas)

1	2
3	4

5	6	7

1. Amitaba 2. Amoghasiddi 3. Ratnasambhava
4. Shakyamuni 5. Chundi 6. Chintamani Chakra
7. Vairocana

Contents

Preface	11
Introduction	13
Part 1: History of Buddhism, and The teachings of the Buddha	17
Historic Buddha Shakyamuni	19
Birth of the Buddha	19
Asita's Prediction	20
The Four Passing Sights	20
The Renunciation	22
The Search	23
The Enlightenment of the Buddha	24
Buddha as the Teacher	26
Mahaprajapati joins the order	27
Buddha's Parinibbana	28
Buddha's Teachings	32
Dukkha, and the Four Noble Truths	32
The Dependent Origins (Pratityasamutpada)	34

Buddha's methods for attaining Nirvana 38

37 Dharma of Enlightenment 38
(Bodhipakkhiyadhamma)

    Four Frames of Reference (Satipatthana) 38
    Four Right Exertions (Sammappadhana) 39
    Four Basis of Power (Iddhipada) 40
    Five Faculties (Indriya) 40
    Five Powers (Bala) 41
    Seven Factors of Enlightenment (Bojjhanga) 42
    Noble Eightfold Path (Ariyo atthangiko maggo) 43

What is Nirvana? 49
What did Buddha mean by "Anatman"? 49
What is enlightenment? 50
Stages of Buddhist attainment 51

Latter Buddhist Developments 54

The First Buddhist Council 54
The Second Buddhist Council 56
The Third Buddhist Council 58
The Fourth Buddhist Council 58

Theravada Buddhism 60

Mahayana Buddhism	62
Early Mahayana Buddhism	62
Madhyamaka	64
Yogacara	65
Vajrayana Buddhism	68
Loss of path to Nirvana	72
What are missing from the scriptures?	75
Was it meant to end this way?	77
A path that was prepared by the Buddha	77
Part 2: The Practice	79
Chundi Buddha Mother	81
Pantheon of Buddhas, and Chundi Buddha	81
Why is Chundi the Buddha to take refuge under?	82
Who is Chundi?	83
Chundi as the Buddha Mother	86
Removal of one's negative Karma	88

The Practice 91

Who this practice is for 91
How to perform the Practice 91

Building relationship with Chundi Buddha 93
Mother, and the Buddhas
How long should this practice be performed ? 93
Practice for the monks 94
Studying the Buddhist scriptures 97

When will I start seeing the results ? 99

What to do when the effect does not take place ? 99
Keeping Moral Precepts 100
When problem persists 101
Chundi's fierce form 103

How to live as a Buddhist 105

Taking on the practice 105
Living a moral life 105
Doing good 107
Building merit 109

The Seven Protector Buddhas of the World — 110

The Seven Buddhas of world protection — 110
Characteristics of the Seven Protector Buddhas — 111

    Chundi — 111
    Shakyamuni — 111
    Amitaba — 112
    Amoghasiddi — 113
    Chintamani Chakra — 113
    Ratnasambhava — 114
    Vairocana — 115

Incorporating Seven Protector Buddha's mantra into daily practice — 115
Making request to Seven Protector Buddhas of the World — 117

Postscript — 118

Path to Nirvana — 118

Bibliography — 119

Preface

Chundi (sometimes spelled Cundi) Buddha Mother is commonly worshipped in Asia, but not well known in the western world. She is a Buddha that appears in the pantheon of Vajirayana Buddhism. What is unique about her is that she is known to be the teacher of both laymen, and monks. Her style of teaching is a combination of direct experience, along with intuitive communications. What is valuable about this teachings is that it fills in the portions of the teachings that is not explained in the agamas (The original teachings of Buddha Shakyamuni). It will take a little while to build relationship with the Buddha Mother, but benefits are worthwhile. This is because through her help, one will be able to enter the path that leads to Nirvana relatively easily.

But, the real benefit of this teachings is the peace, and happiness one gains from taking this path. Most books on religion are like pamphlets at the travel agent's office. It may tell you how nice, and beautiful your destination might be, but when you actually get there, the impression might be entirely different from what was written in the brochure. Same analogy holds with most books written about religion, and spirituality. The problem is, with most religious scriptures, it is only after one's death that one finds out if their claims were true or not. I'm sure everyone will agree that this is not the right time to find out if one's destination meets with their expectations or not. The difference between these practices and the practice written in this book is that one gets to experience the kind of world one's headed to while they are still alive. The peace, and happiness one experiences is very real, and this is one of the few religious books in existence that makes claims as to what results a person can expect within a prescribed number of days. If one finds that their experience does not meet their expectations, one is free to leave the practice after those dates.

You will also have the opportunity to evaluate the rightfulness of the path you are on while you perform the practice. Through these experiences, one can evaluate if the teachings of the Buddha, and the Buddha Mother is true or not. The practice is geared for those who live in the busy modern society, so it is kept simple, and short. Anyone with five minutes of time a day can perform it.

The information necessary to understand the practice will be discussed in the following chapters so anyone can be on their path to Nirvana.

Introduction

There are many books published regarding Buddhism, but they are either oriented towards the academic world, or if they are not, then they are mostly anecdotal words of wisdom, and advise targeted for the laymen. In either case, these books don't contain the practice one can follow that yields actual results.

This book contains both the information necessary to understand the teachings of the Buddha, and also the method of practices that leads to the path to Nirvana. It also provides for attainment of peace, and happiness in one's life that is not merely a state of mind, but manifestation of the power that comes from the practice.

The practice contained in this book is simple, yet powerful. It can be practiced by both laymen, and monks.

This is also one of the few books that states how long the practice needs to be performed before results can be experienced.

This book is written so necessary information can be obtained in the shortest path. The book is written into two sections: The first section contains the history of Buddhism, and the core concept of Buddha's teachings. The second part of the book explains the practice, and what the practitioner may expect from performing these practices.

In the first section, this book presents an overview on how Buddhism came to the present form, along with different schools of thoughts that came about after the Buddha's entry into Nirvana. If the information left in the agamas (scriptures containing original words of the Buddha) were complete, there wouldn't have been the need for later generations to invent new ideas, and practices. But as we will see, explanation regarding certain components of the practice were inexplicable due to them being one's transformation which is a direct result of the practice itself.

In the practice section of this book, how this method can be obtained in a present day will be discussed.

The second section of the book gives detailed description of who Buddha Mother is, and how to perform the practice is shown. The practices are separated into three sections. First part of the practice is for both laymen, and monks. Second part is in regards to meditation Buddha Shakyamuni's disciples were practicing, and this entails direct power transmission from Buddha Mother herself. This is the meditation that was practiced by the Buddha's disciples which is the critical component in the practice to reach Nirvana. Third part of the practice is optional: Buddha Mother works with six other Buddhas on matters involving the entire planet. A disciple may make request on behalf of the world for its betterment. If the request is accepted by the Buddha, those requests will be implemented.

The actual benefit of these practices can only be tried and experienced. This book shows easy method of practice anyone can perform, that also leads to the core teachings of Buddhism.

Part 1:

History of Buddhism, and The teachings of the Buddha

Historic Buddha Shakyamuni

Siddhartha Gautama was born about 583 BCE, in or near what is now Nepal. His father, King Suddhodana, was leader of a clan called the Shakya. His mother, Queen Maya was his wife.

Birth of the Buddha

One day during a midsummer festival, Queen Maya retired to her quarters to rest, and falling asleep, she dreamed a vivid dream. A magnificent white bull elephant bearing six tusks approached, and walked around her three times. Then the elephant entered from the right side, and vanished into her. Soon after Queen Maya noticed that she was pregnant, but was not troubled with any symptoms that usually accompanies pregnancy.

When the time for the birth grew near, Queen Maya wished to wander the Lumbini Grove, which was full of blossoming trees. One day the Queen went to the park to wander about. She found a rare tree, the branches drooping under their burden of blossoms. She went up to it; gracefully extending her hand, she drew down a branch. Suddenly, she stood very still. She smiled, and the maidens who were near her received a lovely child into their arms.

Then the infant stood, took seven steps, and proclaimed " In heavens above, to earth below, I am supreme". The infant was also not defiled by the bodily fluid that accompanies the usual infant birth, and was pure.

Then Queen Maya and her son returned to Kapilavatthu. The Queen died seven days later, and the infant prince was nursed, and raised by the Queen's sister Mahaprajapati.

Asita's Prediction

When Prince Siddhartha was a few days old, a holy man named Asita came to visit the prince. Upon seeing the prince endowed with his 32 marks of excellence, Asita prophesied that the Prince would be a great sage who will set the world free. Then he wept knowing that his time in this world would soon pass, and would not be able to hear the teachings of the Buddha. Although joyed by Asita's words, King Suddhodana feared that the prince will one day renounce the world, so he raised the prince in great luxury and shielded him from the knowledge of human suffering.

The Four Passing Sights

The Prince one day, overcome with curiosity to see the world, asked a charioteer to take him on a ride through the city. On his first tour around the city he saw an old man. The man was leaning on a staff; he was worn out and decrepit. His veins stood out on his body. A few dirty grey hairs hung from his scalp. He gazed at him, and he asked the charioteer:

"What is this man with grey hair and body so bent? Has nature made him thus, or is it chance?"

The charioteer answered: "This is not chance, it is old age. This befalls to everybody."

The prince was deeply moved. He asked: "Will that be my fate, also?"

The charioteer replied: "My lord, youth will also leave you some day and you too, will come to old age."

The prince returned to his palace, and despite his unpleasant experience, he decided to ride once more through the city.

In this trip Siddhartha saw a sick man. He stared at him, and he asked the charioteer: "What is this man with a swollen paunch? He is deathly pale and pitiful cries escape from his lips."

The charioteer answered: "My lord, this man knows the torment of sickness, yet he too, was once healthy and strong."

Prince Siddhartha thought "Men are constantly threatened with sickness. How can they go about their daily life without any concern?"

On his third trip, the prince saw a corpse. He asked the charioteer:

"What is that body doing on the ground?"

The charioteer replied: "My lord, that is a corpse. Life has left his body."

The prince was troubled. He said, "Is this a condition peculiar to this man, or does this same end awaits all creatures?"

And the charioteer answered: "This same end awaits all creatures. Whether of humble or of noble birth, to every being who lives in this world, death comes inevitably."

Siddhartha could no longer find peace. He left the palace on his fourth trip, and as he strolled aimlessly through the country, he saw a man approaching who looked like a beggar. "Who is that?" the prince asked the charioteer.

Charioteer replied: "He is a spiritual aspirant, seeking freedom from this world."

Siddhartha was happy. He saw where his duty lay. He decided to leave the palace and become a monk.

The Renunciation

For a time the Prince returned to palace life, but he took no pleasure in it. Even the news that his wife Yasodhara had given birth to a son did not please him. The child was called Rahula, which means "hindrance"

One night he wandered the palace alone. The luxuries that had once pleased him now seemed grotesque. Musicians and dancing girls had fallen asleep and were sprawled about, snoring and sputtering. Prince Siddhartha reflected on the old age, disease, and death that would overtake them all and turn their bodies to dust.

He realized then that he could no longer be content living the life of a prince. That very night he left the palace, shaved his head, and changed his prince's clothes for a beggar's robe. Then he began his quest for enlightenment.

The Search

Siddhartha began by seeking out renowned teachers, who taught him about the many religious philosophies of his day as well as how to meditate. First teacher was called Arta Kalama. Arta Kalama taught meditation called the realm of no thought, but Shiddhartha after learning this method could not find the release from suffering he was seeking. So he left Arta Kalama to search for another teacher. Second teacher he sought was Uddaka Ramaputta. Uddaka taught meditation called the realm of neither thought or no thought. But after he had learned all he had to teach, his doubts and questions remained. Five disciples of Uddaka left to find enlightenment by themselves, and Siddhartha followed shortly after.

The six companions attempted to find release from suffering through spiritual, and physical practices to their limits. Siddhartha committed himself to extreme austere practice, eating one speck of grain each day. Six years has passed, and yet true knowledge did not come to him. His body has turned into skin, and bones, and he realized that this was not the path to enlightenment.

There was a village called Uruvilva near the spot where Siddhartha was residing. There were ten daughters who revered the hero, and they brought him grain and fruit by way of alms. One of the daughter's name was Sujata. She made rice gruel out of milk that was concentrated over fifty-five cows. She would first milk ten cows, then she would give that milk to nine cows. Then she would milk nine cows, and give those milk to eight cows, until she will milk the last cow, and use that milk to make the rice gruel. Siddhartha accepted this gift, and after nourishing himself, he went, and sat under a banyan tree.

But when he accepted a bowl of rice milk from a young girl, his companions assumed he had given up the quest and they left him and went to Benares.

The Enlightenment of the Buddha

Siddhartha sat beneath a sacred banyan tree, and settled into meditation.

Mara the tempter, sensing that Sidhhartha is about to attain enlightenment, gathered his army, and appeared before Siddhartha. Mara's army attacked with their spears, and arrows, but they all turned into flowers before striking the noble one. Then Mara sent his most beautiful daughter to seduce Siddhartha, but this also failed.

Mara wrung his hands in anguish, and he cried:
"What have I done that this man should defeat me? For they are not a few, those whose desires I have granted! I have often been

kind and generous! Those cowards who are fleeing could bear witness to that."

Whereupon a voice came out of nowhere, and said: "I will be the witness that he is the most generous one."

The voice was that of Mother Earth.

And the Evil One saw a woman of great beauty emerge from the earth, up to her waist. She bowed before the hero, and clasping her hands, she said: "O most holy of men, I bear witness to your generosity."

Then she disappeared.

And Mara, the Evil One, wept because he had been defeated.

That night, in the first watch of the night, he arrived at the knowledge of all that had transpired in previous existences. In the second watch, he learned the present state of all beings. In the third, he understood the dependent origins of life

When dawn appeared, this most noble of men was a Buddha. He exclaimed:

"The mind attains to nirvana; birth is no more for desire is no more.".

Buddha as the Teacher

The Blessed One wondered who was worthy of being the first to hear the word of salvation.

He thought again, and he remembered Uddaka's five disciples who had once joined him. They were virtuous; they were energetic; they would certainly understand the law. The Blessed One knew, by virtue of his intelligence, that Uddaka's five disciples were living in the monastic park at Varanasi. So he set out for Varanasi.

The enlightened one went to the monastic park at Varanasi, located in what is now near the province of Uttar Pradesh. There he found the five companions who had abandoned him, and to them he preached his first sermon. This is known as the first wheel turning of dharma. In this, Buddha taught the middle way that avoid the extremes of pleasure, and self mortification.

Buddha then went to the country of Maghada, and king Bimbisara who met the Buddha prior to his enlightenment gave a gift of Bamboo Grove in his capital city of Rajhagriha. This became the first Vihara or Buddhist monastery. With his teaching center established, and with the support of kings of Magadha, and Kosala, Buddhism spread throughout the region.

During this time, some notable disciples joined the order who would become his chief disciples later on. These included Sariputra, Mogghalana, and Mahakasyapa.

Buddha also taught to laymen, and Anathapindika, a wealthy merchant became his chief lay benefactor. Anathapindika gifted the Buddha with Jetavana vihara which he purchased from prince Jeta in the city of Savatti. Jetavana became the most famous of Buddha's viharas where he gave most of his sermons. A lay woman named Visaka became his chief female benefactor. She also erected a vihara for the Buddha named Migāramātupāsāda near Savatti.

Mahaprajapati joins the order

Mahaprajapati, who was the woman that raised Shiddhartha, came to Ananda who was a cousin and a personal attendant of the Buddha one day and asked to be accepted into the order of monks. Buddha refused Mahaprajapati's request, but she succeeded by soliciting the support of Ananda.

But, one day, the Master said to Ananda:

"If women had not been admitted to the community, Ananda, true teachings would have survived for a thousand years. But now that women are admitted to the community, true teachings will live only five hundred years."

The Buddha devoted himself to teaching, attracting hundreds of followers. Eventually he became reconciled with his father, King Suddhodana. Rahula, his son, became a novice monk at the age of 7 and went on to become an arahant.

Buddha's Parinibbana

Buddha was reaching a ripe old age. When the Buddha reached his eightieth year, he felt that his days in this world were coming to an end. In this last year of his life, he decided to go to Kusinara, a small village in northern India as the place to enter Nirvana. By this time, venerable Yasodhara had already passed away, and so had the Buddha's two chief disciples, venerable Moggallana and venerable Sariputta.

There was one teaching which the Buddha gave again and again during the many stops on his last journey. It was a sermon on the fruits of following the three divisions of the Noble Eightfold Path — morality, concentration and wisdom — which would help his disciples put an end to all sufferings.

When the Buddha and his disciples arrived at Pava, the son of the village goldsmith, whose name was Cunda, invited the party to a meal that would later be known as the sukaramaddava, or "boar food".

The Buddha advised everyone not to touch the sukaramaddava that Cunda had prepared, and claimed "Only the Buddha may eat such a food.". Buddha proclaimed "I do not see anyone in the world other than the Blessed One who could digest such food." The other food that Cunda had prepared could be served to the other monks. But soon after this, the Buddha suffered food poisoning. Though extremely weak, the Buddha continued on to Kusinara, ten kilometers away from Cunda's house. After a painful struggle, he reached a grove of sala trees inside the town.

Now it happened that a certain wandering ascetic called Subhadda was staying near Kusinara and, hearing that the Buddha was about to pass away, he resolved to go and see him. Subhadda had a question he could not resolve and was sure that the Buddha could answer his question and clear his doubts.

With Buddha's permission, Subhadda approached him, and after greeting him, said, "O Gotama, what are the difference between your teachings, and the teachings of other teachers ?"

"O Subhadda," said the Buddha, "You have asked the question, and now I will tell you the truth."

"In whatever doctrine or teaching where the 37 Dharma of Enlightenment is not found, there will neither be found those who have become sotapanna, sakadagami, anagami or arahant (four levels of sainthood). Only in the teaching of the Buddha, O Subhadda, is to be found the 37 Dharma of Enlightenment, and in it alone the sotapanna, the sakadagami, the anagami, and the arahant are found. In no other schools of religious teachers can such arya beings (saints) be found."

In this way Subhadda became the very last convert, and disciple of the Buddha.

Then the Buddha, addressing the other monks said, "If any amongst you has any questions as to the Buddha's teachings, ask me now so that afterwards you will have no regrets that you did not ask me while I was still with you."

But at these words, none of the monks said anything. None had any questions, and all of them were silent. Then the Buddha said, "Perhaps it may be out of respect for the teacher, that you do not question me. Let a friend, O disciples, tell it to another friend so he may ask me the question for you." Still the disciples remained silent.

Then venerable Ananda spoke to the Buddha, "It is wonderful. It is marvelous, Lord! I do believe that in all this great company of monks there is not a single one who has doubts or questions about the Buddha, the teaching or the order of monks, or the path and the method of training and conduct."

"That is true Ananda," said the Buddha, "not one single monk gathered here has any doubt or question about these things. Of all the 500 monks here, Ananda, he who is the most backward is a sotapanna, not subject to fall back to a lower state of existence, but is certain and destined for enlightenment."

Then the Buddha addressed all the monks once more, and these were the very last words he spoke:

"O monks, this is my advice to you. All things in this world are changeable. They are not lasting. After the Buddha is gone, you must become your own light. Put an unyielding effort to gain your own salvation."

Then the Buddha lapsed into the jana stages, or meditative absorptions. Going from level to level, one after the other, ever deeper and deeper. Then he came out of the meditative absorption for the last time and passed into Nirvana, leaving nothing whatever behind that can cause rebirth again in this or any other world.

The passing away of the Buddha, occurred in 543 BC on a full-moon day in the month of May, known in the Indian calendar as Vesak.

After the Parinibbana of the Buddha, his body was cremated. Then the relics were given by arahat Khema to king Brahmadatta for veneration.

Buddha's relic traveled around Southeast Asian countries over the ages, and they can now be found in countries like Sri Lanka, India, China, and Japan.

Buddha's Teachings

Dukkha, and the Four Noble Truths

Following are what Buddha considered as Dukkha or suffering. The realization of the existence of these sufferings were prince Siddhartha's reason for taking on the monastic life, and are the basic tenets of Buddhism. Life is suffering, and therefore we take the road to salvation. First four are the basic suffering due to existence, and the second are the suffering experienced during one's life.

> Life is suffering
> Sickness is suffering
> Old age is suffering
> Death is suffering
>
> Getting what one doesn't want is suffering
> Not getting what one wants is suffering
> Not being able to hold on to what one loves is suffering
> Not being able to control one's mind and body is suffering

Buddha also expounded on the Four Noble Truths, which are:

> Truth on suffering
> Truth on origin of suffering
> Truth on cessation of suffering
> Truth on the path that leads to the cessation of suffering

The first of the four noble truth the "Truth of Suffering" is explained in the Dukkhas mentioned above. The second truth on the origin of suffering is called Pratītyasamutpāda or dependent origins, and is important in understanding the origins of human suffering. Buddha's thesis was that since there is a depend origins to things that are born into this world, things change when the dependent conditions change. Understanding in Buddhism is that because of these changes, aforementioned suffering occurs.

In the following sections, Buddha's methods for attaining liberation from sufferings will be explained. Buddha's practice leading to the cessation of suffering is based on slowing down of the effects of the force that causes dependent origin to continue, and to develop powers to transcend the world of existence. Dependent origins is a sequence of desire and cognitions that forms a loop, which can go on forever. Unfortunately good translation of this doctrine is difficult to find, and has become one of the most misrepresented concepts in Buddhism. Dependent origins should first be understood from the view point of how our life springs into existence. The concept behind this is that there's a fine substance that obeys the will of a person which forms the basis of the creation of life.

Dependent origins will be explained in the following section from the stand point of how desire moves the will to create life. Because there is life, there is death, and if this cycle can be broken, death will cease to exist.

Buddha has spoke of this when he became enlightened, and exclaimed:

"I have seen you at last, O builder of the house (body). You no longer build the house. The rafters are broken; the old walls are down. The ancient mountain crumbles; the mind attains to nirvana; birth is no more for desire is no more."

The fourth element of the Four Noble Truth, "The path that leads to the cessation of suffering." is also given in the following section. This is called the 37 Dharma of Enlightenment (Bodhipakkhiyadhamma).

Bodhipakkhiyadhamma is another concept in Buddhism that has often been misrepresented. It has commonly been reduced to "The Noble Eightfold Path", where in fact the Noble Eightfold Path is only a small portion of Bodhipakkhiyadhamma. Bodhipakkhiyadhamma is a collection of discipline that is designed to gain the power to attain Nirvana. The difficulty in directly using the 37 Dharma of Enlightenment is in that how to practice some of its methods has been lost to history, and are no longer available to us. How to overcome this lack of information will be explained in the section regarding the practice.

The Dependent Origins (Pratītyasamutpāda)

Pratītyasamutpāda consists of the following twelve sequences of events.

1. Avidya (Ignorance)

> Desires from the past: What created all the desires is ignorance, so ignorance is used as the representative word.

2. From Avidya, Samskara (That which has been put together) arises

> This points to the aggregate inertia of deeds from the past, that has been caused by one's desires.

3. From Samskara, Vijnana (Life force, mind, and discernment) arises

> The inertia now forms the spiritual body, and consciousness within the mother's womb.

4. From Vijnana, Namarupa (Mind and body) arises

> Physical body, its sensation, perception, mental action, and discernment takes shape within the mother's womb.

5. From Namarupa, Sadayatana (Six sense basis) arises

> With the growth of Namarupa, vision, hearing, olfaction, taste, touch, and thought forms, along with desire to exit the womb.

6. From Sadayatana, Sparsa (Touch sense) arises

Short period after birth, the new born begins to sense the world around it through touch senses.

7. From Sparsa, Vedana (Perception) arises

After the five senses starts working, affinity to pleasure, and aversion to discomfort occurs.

8. From Vedana, Trsna (Thirst) arises

As part of the development of the senses, thirst for what is loved or coveted arises, including the rise of sexual desire during pubity.

9. From Trsna, Upadana (Grasping) arises

From love, desire to attain what is loved arises.

10. From Upadana, Bhava (Continuity of life) arises

Desire invokes inertial action that creates the cause of next life.

11. From Bhava, Jati (Birth) arises

From the inertial action, future birth occurs.

12. From Jati, Jaramarana (Old age, and death) arises

Old age, and death arises as the inertia which created Vijnana slows and comes to a halt.

Here I use the word inertia which is a modern term that didn't exist during the time of the Buddha. But it's appropriate in that it describes the law of nature that action performed presently can carry into the future. This points to the existence of a matter that is yet to be discovered by science, but as much part of this universe as material objects. Like objects forged by physical force, this matter is forged by mental action, and retains its property until it wears out just like physical objects. Modern science has just started to look into these matters starting with study of chi. Chi is called ki in Japanese, and prana by the Indians. It is a matter that is half ways between physical matter, and mind. It follows the command of one's mind and will, and can show effect on materials in the physical world. It is not yet clear how these matters act in the creation of life, but it is a component of substances that are involved in the formation of life.

Buddha's methods for attaining Nirvana

37 Dharma of Enlightenment (Bodhipakkhiyadhamma)

Buddhism is consistent in its world view, and practice in that the rules monks obey, are designed to attenuate the inertial force of this substance that creates our mind, and sensation.

There is a collection of practice Buddha's disciples followed in what is known as Bodhipakkhiyadhamma or what is called 37 Dharma of Enlightenment in english. By following this practice, monks were able to gradually lose their hindrances, and gain power to attain Nirvana.

Some of Bodhipakkhiyadhamma's practices such as the Eightfold Noble Path is well known, but others are not so well known, and still others are difficult to understand. But Buddha considered these all essential to attaining Nirvana. The 37 Dharma of Enlightenment consists of the following seven groups that forms 37 areas of practices.

Four Frames of Reference (Satipatthana)

Contemplation of the body

To understand that our body is impure

Contemplation of feelings

To understand that senses are suffering

Contemplation of consciousness

To understand that our consciousness is ever changing

Contemplation of mental qualities

To understand that there is no ego

Four Right Exertions (Sammappadhana)

Exertion for the non-arising of unskillful states

Effort to prevent undesirable qualities from arising

Exertion for the abandoning of unskillful states

Effort to do away with undesirable qualities

Exertion for the arising of skillful states

Effort to promote desirable qualities

Exertion for the sustaining of skillful states

Effort to keep desirable qualities

Four Basis of Power (Iddhipada)

Will

Will to attain better meditation

Energy

Energy to attain better meditation. Avoids laziness.

Consciousness

Ability to focus consciousness

Discrimination

Use of discrimination to attain better meditation

Five Faculties (Indriya)

Faith

Faith in Buddha's teachings

Energy

> *Exertion towards four right exertions*

Mindfulness

> *Focus on the Four Frames of Reference*

Concentration

> *Achieving the four Dhyanas*

Wisdom

> *Discerning the Four Noble Truths*

Five Powers (Bala)

Faith

> *Controls Doubt*

Energy

> *Controls laziness*

Mindfulness

Concentration
    Controls heedlessness

    Controls distraction

Wisdom

    Controls ignorance

Seven Factors of Enlightenment (Bojjhanga)

Mindfulness

    Mindful of the Dharma

Investigation

    Investigation of Dharma

Energy

    To put effort into one's practice

Joy

    Joy that arises from performing the practice

Tranquility

Tranquility of body and mind

Concentration

Concentration in meditation

Equanimity

Meet life with detachment and calmness

Noble Eightfold Path (Ariyo atthangiko maggo)

In the early Pali texts, Noble Eightfold Path was considered a part of Bodhipakkhiyadhamma, and not considered a stand alone practice as it is today.

Right View (samma ditti)

Right view is the core concept behind the Noble Eightfold Path, and it is actualized by practicing the remaining seven path of the Noble Eightfold Path. In this sense, all of the Noble Eightfold Path is inclusive within the Right View. This is explained in Samaditti Sutta (Majjhima Nikaya 9). Right View is also the wisdom where the Four Noble Truth originates. There are also the following branches of Right View.

Kammassakatā sammā-diṭṭhi

Kammassaka: Only the wholesome and unwholesome actions of all beings are their own properties that always accompany them wherever they may wander in many a becoming or world-cycle.

Kammadayada: Only the wholesome and unwholesome actions of all beings are their inherited properties that always accompany them wherever they may wander in many a becoming or world-cycle.

Kammayoni: Only the wholesome and unwholesome actions of beings are the origin of their wanderings in many a becoming or world-cycle.

Kammabadhu: Only the wholesome and unwholesome actions of beings are their relatives and true friends that always accompany them wherever they may wander in many a becoming or world-cycle.

Kammappatisarana: Only the wholesome and unwholesome actions of beings are their real refuge wherever they may wander in many a becoming or world-cycle.

Dasavatthuka Samma-ditthi

Atthi dinnam: There really exists alms-giving (dana) as cause (kamma) and its result (vipaka)

Atthi yittham: There really exists offering on a large scale as cause and its result.

Atthi hutam: There really exists offering on a small scale as cause and its result.

Atthi sukata dukkatanam kammanam phalam vipako: There really exist wholesome and unwholesome actions as causes and their results.

Atthi mata: There really exist the good and the evil deeds done to one's mother as causes and their results.

Atthi pita: There really exist the good and the evil deeds done to one's father as causes and their results.

Atthi sata opapatika: There really exist beings who are born by apparitonal rebirth such as beings in purgatory, petas, devas, sakkas and Brahmas who cannot ordinarily be seen by men.

Atthi ayamloko: There really exists this world which is under our very eyes.

Atthi paroloko: There really exist the other worlds or planes where one may arise after death. In another way, there really exists this human world (ayamloko) and there really exists the other worlds (paroloko: four lower worlds, six deva worlds and twenty Brahma worlds).

In another way, there really exists this universe consisting of the human world, four lower worlds, six deva worlds and twenty

Brahma worlds (ayamloko); and there really exist other worlds which are infinite in all eight directions (paroloko).

Atthi loke samanabrahmana samaggata samma patipanna ye imanca lokam paranca lokam sayam abhinna sacchikatva pavedenti: There really exist, in this human world, persons like the Omniscient Buddha, monks and brahmins who practice the True Dhamma and possess tranquility of mind and who, having seen and realized this very world and other worlds through their own insight, impart their knowledge to others.

Catu-sacca Samma-ditthi

1. Dukkhe nanam: Penetrative insight into the Truth of Suffering.
2. Dukkha samudaye nanam: Penetrative insight into the Truth of the Origin of Suffering.
3. Dukkha nirodhe nanam: Penetrative insight into the Truth of the Cessation of Suffering.
4. Dukkha nirodhagaminipatipaddya nanam: Penetrative insight into the Truth of the Path Leading to the Cessation of Suffering.

Right Intention (samma sankappa)

Right intention is to correctly consider, and decide one's action from a Buddhistic context. Three major areas of Right Intentions are:

Detachment from worldliness (nekkama sankappa): To be detached, and maintain detachment from worldly object of desire such as fame, wealth, social status, and five sense desires.

Detachment from anger (abiyapada sankappa): To intend detachment from anger.

Detachment from harming others (avihimsa sankappa): To intend detachment from harming others including all living beings.

Right Speech (samma vaca)

Right speech consists of abstinence from lying, divisive speech, abusive speech, and idle chatter.

Right Action (samma kammanta)

Right Action consists of abstinence from harming others, abstinence from stealing, and abstinence from immoral actions.

Right Livelihood (samma ajiva)

Right Livelihood means a practitioner should not engage in occupation that may directly, or indirectly harm others.

Right Effort (samma vayama)

Right Effort is to put one's energy, and efforts into the following four areas:

Effort to prevent evil or unskillful qualities to arise.
Abandonment of unskillful or evil that have arisen.
Effort to arise skillful or good qualities.
Effort to maintain good, and skillful qualities that has arisen.

Right Mindfulness (samma sati)

Right Mindfulness is being aware or maintaining vigilance over one's condition of body, sense, mind, and Dharma.

Right Concentration (samma samadhi)

Right Concentration is synonymous to right meditation, and together with Right Mindfulness, one is able to arrive at Right View.

Asides from these spiritual practices, monks had to adhere to code of conduct called Pratimoksa. In Theravada Buddhism there are 227 rules for the monks, and 311 for the nuns. Many of these rules are only relevant to ordained monks and nuns, and are not applicable to laymen (such as rules about how to accept new monk's robes etc.). These are part of what is called Vinaya or discipline, and has its history in rules set by the Buddha in his sangha.

What is Nirvana ?

Buddha's teaching was that the substance that carries our deeds, and desires, can be slowed down, and in the end what creates one's existence in this universe can be made to come to a halt. The calming action in sanskrit is called nirvata, and from it comes the word Nirvana.

From this, it can be seen that Nirvana is not a description of a place, or a world, but a state that is reached after all the inertia that creates our mind, and body has come to a stop.

What did Buddha mean by "Anatman" ?

Buddha has stated that there is no "Self (Atman)" or spirit that transmigrates forever. Then the question remains, what is left after one reaches Nirvana ? If nothing remains, then obviously one's existence will be wiped out from this universe, and yet, Buddha and his arahant disciples remained on this earth until their physical body has run its course. Then there must be something else that allows for consciousness to continue.

During his time on earth, Buddha has spoken about the existence of Buddha nature, or Buddha consciousness (Tathagatha garba) that exists in all beings. This is the pure, complete consciousness that is without any lack, and is always in eternal bliss. It is this Buddha nature that remains after one reaches Nirvana. Buddha nature is a complete consciousness that this entire universe is only a small subset of.

In the yogacara school of Mahayana Buddhism, a first written record of what is called the alaya consciousness was introduced. Alaya consciousness is the eighth consciousness, and is called alaya (warehouse) because it contains everything. Tathagatha garba (Buddha consciousness) and alaya consciousness is one and the same, and can be reached through Buddhist practice.

What causes our existence in this universe are formed out of materials in this universe. Even our mind is formed out of substance that exists in this universe. Everything that exists in this universe are subject to change, and from this reason, Buddha has stated that there is no unchanging entity that transmigrates (Anatman). In modern terms this means there is no such thing as a soul that transmigrates.

This may cause some disagreement from religion that base its practice on the discovery of "self". But there should be a distinction between "Atman", and "Paramatman" where atman is the self that forms the person, and paramatman which is one and the same with Tathagatha garba (Buddha nature).

What is enlightenment ?

If you've read up to this point, you've probably noticed something. That is there should be another Pratītyasamutpāda that deals with how the consciousness that's outside of this universe have interacted with the elements of this universe to form our mind, and the senses. How something that was complete got entangled with the universe is a mystery, but it has happened, and that is why we are here. Tathagatha garba is subtlest of the subtle, and will not be detected until one has attained quiescence of mind, and inertial action from the past has nearly stopped. Enlightened ones are the ones who've seen their own Tathagatha garba.

But there's one question that remains in Pratītyasamutpāda in that how the link between the Tathagatha garba, and the mind can be broken. This final step from what I understand requires external assistance by a Buddha or an arhat.

After passing of the Buddha, arhats would help the junior disciples to attain Nirvana, but as number of arhats waned in the sangha, the method to break the final link became lost.

Stages of Buddhist attainment

Buddhism divides stages to enlightenment into four stages. Each stage is attributed to the amount of fetters one has managed to eradicate. These four stages occur in the following order.

Stream Winner (Sotapanna)

By eradicating the first three fetters, an aspirant enters the path, and becomes a Stream Winner. The three lower fetters being eradicated are:

1. Identity View - Believing that Self exists
2. Skeptical Doubt - Doubt towards Buddha's teachings
3. Clinging to rites, and rituals - Believing that performing these will result in favorable outcome

When one becomes a Stream winner, within next seven rebirths, one will attain Nirvana.

Once Returner (Sakadagami)

By eradicating the first three fetters, and significantly reducing the next two fetters, one becomes a Once Returner. The two additional fetters weakened are:

1. Craving
2. Ill will

Once returner returns once more to the human world unless they attain never returner status in a heavenly realm, which in case they will attain enlightenment in another world, and will not return to the world of humans.

Never returner (Anagami)

By eradicating the first five fetters, one becomes a non returner. Because craving has been eradicated, one no longer is born into the desire realm which the human world is a part of. When one becomes a never returner, one is reborn into a pure abode, and from there they attain enlightenment.

Arhat

Arhat or Arahant is one who've attained Nirvana. It is one of the ten titles of a Buddha, and means "One worthy of offerings". Arhats have eradicated all ten fetters, and are enjoying Nirvana while their physical body may still exist in this world. The five higher fetters they've eradicated are:

1. Desire to be reborn into physical world
2. Desire to be reborn into subtile world
3. Conceit
4. Restlessness
5. Ignorance

Out of all these attainment, the most important is to become a Stream Winner. Why ? because once you become a Stream Winner, all the rest follows automatically. But before one attains the status of a Stream Winner, one can be a Bodhisattva where the chances of leaving the path becomes greatly diminished.

Latter Buddhist Developments

Although Buddhism is well known to the public, it is not so well known that school of thoughts in Buddhism are not monolithic, and shows evolution it went through over the ages. It's important to recognize which period of Buddhism each sect represents in order to put their school of thought into perspective.

Order of monks started to break apart around 100 years after Buddha's parinibbhana. This spawned Mahayana Buddhism, and various other schools of Buddhist thoughts.

The First Buddhist council

Shortly after the Buddha's parinibbhana, first meeting was held to preserve his teachings.

Understandably, the Buddha's parinibbhana was a great loss to most of his followers, except for the deeply realized disciples, and many were plunged into deep grief. Yet there was a monk who entered the order in his old age, that rejoiced at the Buddha's disappearance.

"Do not be sad, brothers," he said. "We are now free of the Great Ascetic who constantly admonished us, saying 'This is suitable, this is not suitable.' Now we are free from him."

These unexpected words spoken by a monk hardly a week after the parinibbhana of the Buddha caused Venerable Maha Kassapa, the third chief disciple of the Buddha, to call a meeting of the leading arahants in order to protect and preserve the teachings. Other elder monks were consulted and they all welcomed this suggestion.

King Ajatasattu was informed of the intention of the order of Monks and he made all necessary arrangements for the monks to meet at the entrance of the Sattapanni Cave in Rajagaha. Five hundred seats were arranged and prepared in the large hall, but only 499 famous arahants were chosen for the meeting. The empty seat was reserved for the Venerable Ananda, who was still only a sotapanna. Ananda exerted himself in his practice, and on the night before the meeting he attained enlightenment, and became an arhat.

The meeting started three months after the passing away of the Buddha. That meeting is now referred to as the First Buddhist Council.

The Venerable Maha Kassapa was the president at the First Council. Venerable Upali was chosen to answer questions about the vinaya, the monks' and nuns' disciplinary rules. Venerable, Ananda who had the honor of hearing all the discourses of the Buddha and who had an unusually good memory, was chosen to recite all the discourses and answer questions about the teachings.

The First Buddhist Council collected together and arranged the Buddhist Scriptures known as the Pali Tipitaka.

It took monks more than twenty one months to recite the whole of the Vinaya and the Dhamma and those monks sufficiently endowed with good memories retained all that had been recited.

The Second Buddhist Council

The Second Buddhist council took place approximately one hundred years after the Buddha's parinibbhana. Schism in the sangha between the Sthaviras and what was called the Mahasamghikas became obvious during the course of this council.

By this time, Buddhist sangha or the order of monks was divided into two groups. First was the Sthaviras, or the "Elders" that held on to the tradition of laws according to the teachings of the Buddha, and Mahasamghikas literally meaning "The Great Sangha" or the great assembly of monks who were probably in a submissive role to the Sthaviras as students or novices within the order of monks. Mahasamghikas is significant in that they probably were the progenitors of Mahayana Buddhism. The schism between these two groups amongst other things were over vinaya or rules monks must obey. Mahasamghikas requested relaxation of ten different rules in vinaya be made. These ten items were permission to:

1. Store salt for later use.
2. Eat after sun's shadow has passed midday by two finger width.
3. Eat more than once a day.
4. Hold the Uposatha Ceremony with monks dwelling in the same locality.
5. Carry out official acts before the assembly has ratified it.
6. Follow a certain practice because it was done by one's tutor or teacher.
7. Eat sour milk after one had his midday meal.
8. Consume fruit drink after it has fermented and turned into alcohol.
9. Use a sitting rug.
10. Accept gold and silver as alms.

The Elders rejected these changes. Perhaps there were more fundamental schism that existed between the elders, and the lay monks in that the elders were keeping the teachings to themselves. Elders were the keepers of the Buddha's original teachings, and they might not have been shared openly with other monks. This special privilege held by the elders may have triggered a dissension between the two parties. This was the first split in school of thoughts in Buddhism, and the two groups never merged together again.

Third Buddhist Council

The Third Buddhist council was convened around 250 BCE at Asokarama in Pataliputra. The reason for convening the Third Buddhist Council was to rid the sangha of corruption and bogus monks.

The cause for this had its origin in patronage of emperor Asoka who generously provided food, and clothing for the monks. This attracted those who's only purpose for joining the order was to gain benefits from the emperor's generosity. So it was that in the fifteenth year of the Emperor Asoka's reign the Third Council was called. One thousand monks from the sixty thousand participants were chosen for the recitation of the Dhamma, which went on for nine months. Those who held wrong views were exposed and expelled from the sangha immediately. In this way the sangha was purged of bogus monks.

The Fourth Buddhist Council

Fourth Buddhist Council is the name of two separate Buddhist council meetings. The first one was held in 29 BC, in Sri Lanka under the patronage of King Vattagamani. This was held in response to a year in which the harvests in Sri Lanka were particularly poor, and many monks subsequently died of starvation. Because Pali Canon was in that time solely remembered by heart, surviving monks recognized the danger of not writing the teachings of the Tipitaka down, so that even if some of the monks (whose duty it was to study and remember parts of the Tipitaka for later generations) died, the teachings would not be lost. This Fourth Buddhist Council took three years.

The second Fourth Buddhist Council was held in Jalandhar around the 1st century BCE. This council amongst other things, put extensive commentaries on the Sarvastivadin (One of the major sect of Theravada Buddhism) Abbidharma into writing. These commentaries were made by Mahayana Buddhists, and was critical of the beliefs Sarvastivadin Abbidharma had held.

Theravada Buddhism

Theravada Buddhism has its roots in the Buddha's original sangha (sanscrit samgha: meaning - order of monks). It is the oldest surviving branch of Buddhism. Theravada means "The Teaching of the Elders".

During the second Buddhist council, according to Theravada tradition, Theravada monks walked out of the council because of the dispute that could not be resolved between them and the Mahasanghikas. The split in sangha was permanent, and Theravada, and Mahayana (which is believed to be started by a group within the Mahasamghikas) will go their separate way, and develop independently from that point on.

During the time of king Asoka, Theravada Buddhism reached Sri Lanka, and from there it spread to Thai, Laos, Cambodia, and Myanmar. While the Theravada spread to the southeast of India, Mahayana Buddhism spread north east of India toward Tibet, China, Korea, and Japan.

In the early stages of Mahayana Buddhism, Mahayana school criticizing the scriptures written by a part of Theravada school called the Sarvastivadin. But this rivalry between the two schools seemed to have contributed to the growth of early Mahayana scriptures. In the later Mahayana Buddhism, Yogacara school started incorporating ideas from the Abbidharma studies of the Theravada schools.

Theravada schools maintains the closest form of sangha to the original Shakyamuni's order of monks. Theravada Buddhism also has advanced studies in meditation techniques.

Theravada Buddhism is important in that they still retain the Vinaya or the rules monks must obey in their practice in relatively pristine condition. While Mahayana, and Vajrayana Buddhism has their own rules for the monks, many are not as close to the original rules followed by the monks in Buddha Shakyamuni's time as in Theravada Buddhism.

Mahayana Buddhism

Mahayana Buddhism was believed to have started shortly after the time of the Second Buddhist council.

Mahayana Buddhism as a whole has three distinct periods of development.

First period introduced the idea of Prajinaparameta,

Second period introduced the philosophy of Madhyamaka

Third period is represented by the appearance of yogacara school of thought

Early Mahayana Buddhism

The word Mahayana first appeared in Prajinaparamita Sutra, and Mahayana Buddhism is thought to have its origin with the group that wrote these texts. Prajinaparamita mean "Great Wisdom", and this school of thought put forth the idea of sunya or "emptiness" to explain Buddha's concept. It is thought that the underlying reason for the Mahayana group to feature this philosophy is to criticize the Sarvastivadin's (A branch of Theravada which formed a major group) idea that Dharma has reality, and exists indefinitely.

Mahayana means great vehicle, and its name suggests a great vehicle that will take the masses to Nirvana. True to its name, early Mahayana scriptures such as Sukhaavatiivyuuha (Infinite Life Sutra) introduced Amitaba Buddha who's vow was to allow anyone who recites his name ten times, and holds on to the Buddhist dharma into his paradise. In this way, early Mahayana Buddhism allowed laymen to enter into Buddha's paradise without long period of practice.

While these claims has no basis in reality, it is significant that concept of opening the passage to the mass to attain Nirvana was introduced for the first time in Buddhism.

Mahayana schools also introduced the concept that other Buddhas who've attained Nirvana in the past are still at work in this world to help the masses. In this, they've created their own world view where Buddhas other than Shakyamuni plays their role in helping the practitioner attain Nirvana.

These scriptures were written by the Mahayana group and not connected to the actual words of the Buddha. What made the confusion worse was that these sutras often started with the verse "Thus have I heard" like the ones that were written by their Theravada predecessors, making the distinction between them difficult.

Madhyamaka

In the 2nd century, second major philosophical school in Mahayana Buddhism, the Madhyamaka was founded. Madhyamaka's philosophy was based on the dependent origin idea put forth by the Buddha - that there is nothing that exists independently by itself. Madhyamaka means "Middle way", and this concept is also related to Buddha's philosophy, that things are neither deterministic, or random, but has dependent cause and effect. Madhyamaka is also called Sunyavada, and incorporates the concept of "Sunya" or emptiness of earlier Mahayana Buddhism into its philosophy.

The text Mūlamadhyamakakārikā (Fundamental verses on the middle way) written by Nagarjuna was the first major scholastic Mahayana sutras that applied detailed analysis on various nature of human, and worldly existence. The rivalry between Theravada, and Mahayana schools still seemed to be strong when Nagarjuna wrote this text, and while taking on similar analytical approach to the nature of reality, there is a fundamental criticism against Sarvastivadin Theravada Abbidharma school of thoughts in his text.

Concept of sunya was still a major part of this school's philosophy, and it might be seen that Madhyamika (those who practice Madhyamaka) extended the earlier Prajinaparamita concept. While these new sutras and schools of thoughts appeared, it was still lacking in that they couldn't show a practicable way of attaining Nirvana.

Yogacara

Further studies by individual practitioner lead to the birth of Yogacara school of Buddhism in the fifth century. Yogacara as the name suggests, the practitioners used yoga to explore deeper into their meditation. Their claim was that everything in this world was a product of consciousness, and in fact the only thing that exists is consciousness itself (Vijnapti-matrata).

Yogacara's criticism of Madhyamaka school was that if nothing exists independently, then what (is the force that) recognizes them as existence ? Yogacara's thesis was that a part of consciousness forms an ego which in tern sees things outside of it as separate existence, and both the idea of self (ego) and the world around it comes from consciousness, therefore there's nothing that exists asides from consciousness.

Yogacara introduced the concept of alaya vijnana (store-house consciousness). Word alaya means store-house, and it is so called because it contains all consciousness.
Alaya vijnana is the eighth consciousness after the eyes, nose, ear, mouth, touch, thought, and manas (self) consciousness. Because it is the root consciousness of all phenomena, it is also called the all seed consciousness (sarva bijaka vijnana). In Lankavatara sutra, alaya consciousness is said to be same as the Tathagata Garva (Buddha consciousness).

The founding of this school is credited to one who's name is Maitreya. There's some historical debates as to who Maitreya was. Yagacarin school was first brought forth by brothers

Asanga, and Vasubandhu. Tales of Asanga tells about him making a trip to Tushita heaven, and asking the future Buddha Maitreya to come down to earth, and give series of lectures. According to his account, this Maitreya is the future Buddha Maitreya. Due to the fantastic nature of this claim, there are other speculations as to who Maitreya was. One is that there was a Buddhist teacher named Maitreya that gave the lecture, and another is that it was Asanga himself who gave the lecture as Maitraya.

* * * *

By the time Mahayana Buddhism reached China, all of the above distinctions were lost, and Buddhism was absorbed as a whole. All the scriptures were taken as the authentic teachings of Buddha Shakyamuni. Buddhism east of China were all affected by this misunderstanding, and until the modern era, Buddhism of Vietnam, Korea, and Japan believed that Mahayana Buddhism was the authentic teachings of the Buddha. Throughout the ages, Mahayana Buddhism split into many sect depending on the particular sutra they specialized their studies in. Then further divisions amongst each sect occurred, and now there are literally hundreds of major, and minor Buddhist sects throughout east Asia.

Modern day Mahayana Buddhism has morphed significantly from the traditional Buddhism, and many Mahayana monks are married, has a family, and operates their temple as a business. In India, there is a concept called Grihastha Ashram or one's house is a temple. Many modern day Mahayana monks seems to take this path where they engage in the four different areas of Grihasta Ashram activity, namely Dharma (religious principles), Artha (economic development), Kama (sense gratification), and Moksha (liberation). Grihasta Ashrams are considered householders in Hinduism, and are not considered to be monks. In this respect it is questionable whether the gathering of such Mahayana monks should still be considered a sangha, because they would have fell under the householder classification in Buddha's time.

Vajrayana Buddhism

The three great movements of Mahayana Buddhism, came to an end in India by the beginning of 6th century, and Buddhism takes another turn in direction. The new direction put Virocana or the Sun Buddha at the center of the pantheon along with Buddhas that represents various aspects of Buddhist teachings and power. This new movement was called Vajirayana from the verse in its seminal text Vajirasekhara Sutra. This new Buddhism was a departure in that they stressed once again the teachings needs to be directly transmitted by the master to his disciples. In this way Buddhism has come a full circle from being a practice for professional monks to teachings for the masses, and once again practice for professional monks. There's a debate about whether Vajirayana Buddhism is part of Mahayana Buddhism or not. Traditionally, Vajirayana Buddhist of Tibet considers themselves separate from the Mahayana movement, but Vajrayana Buddhist of Japan considers themselves part of the Mahayana tradition.

Due to the secret nature of its teachings, Vajrayana Buddhism was not well known to the public in most countries.

Vajrayana Buddhism is known for the usage of mantra in most of its practices. In Vajrayana Buddhism it is used extensively in connecting with various aspects of its practice. In Tibetan Buddhism, Buddhism is separated into Prajinaparamitayana which is the traditional exoteric Mahyana Buddhism, and Mantrayana which is the esoteric Vajrayana Buddhism.

Mantrayana means mantra vehicle, and points to the fact that it uses mantra at the core of its practice.

Another practice employed by Vajrayana Buddhism is the usage of mudra (spiritual hand posture). Mudra is used to symbolize the object of focus of the practice. The purpose of using mudra, and mantra is to control the components of one's volition. The three faculties of human volition is intent, words, and physical act. By focusing the mind, reciting the mantra, and forming the mudra, the practitioner is in control of all three faculties of volition. This helps to keep the focus of the practitioner's intent on the task.

According to the noted Vajrayana scholar Buton Rinchen Drub, Vajrayana Buddhism began its history in the second to the sixth century in India. It believed that initially Vajrayana Buddhism started by Buddhists experimenting with the tantric practice from their locality.

It is in its second developmental period in the seventh century that Vajrayana Buddhism came on its own. Several notable sutras (such as Vajrasekhara Sutra, Mahavairocana Tantra etc.) were written around this time which became the foundation of Vajrayana teachings. The central concept that came about during this time was that Vairocana who is the primeval Buddha taught these teachings. The teachings are separated into practice, and the explanations pertaining to thereof. It is understood that the practice is not effective until one receives the knowledge behind it. The rule was that knowledge is to be transmitted from teacher to student, and should not be taught to the uninitiated.

During this period, concept of Mandala appeared in the scriptures. Mandala of the Womb Realm (Gharbhakosa-dhatu), and Diamond Realm (Vajra-Dhatu), are two main mandala from this period. The two mandalas contain's number of Buddhas, and Bodhisattvas. Each Buddha or Bodhisattvas has unique character that is said to aid the practitioner on their path.

By the appearance of Vajrayana sutras, Vajrayana Buddhism constructed their own system of teachings, and practices that sets them apart from other branches of Buddhism.

Vajrayana Buddhism reached China around eighth century, and spread to Japan, and Korea in subsequent years. Arrival of Vajrayana scholars from India also accelerated the growth of Vajrayana in China.

Third and the final phase of Vajrayana Buddhism came about in the eighth century. The Vajrayana Buddhism of this period takes another turn in its teachings.

The scriptures of this period is no longer called the sutras, and instead are called tantras. Tantras from this period are called Anuttarayogatantra (Supreme Union Tantra) by the Tibetans. Tantric Buddhist texts started arriving in Tibet and China around the eleventh century.

In Tibet, Atisa, a highly trained monk arrived from India, and this helped to root Vajrayana Buddhism in Tibet. Tibetan Buddhism is important in that due to Islamic invasion into India, late Vajrayana Buddhism never reached China. But due to its close proximity to India, it did reach Tibet, and was translated word for word into their language. For this reason, Tibetan scriptures hold high value from scholastic standpoint.

In the 14th century, Kagyu, and Sakya sect introduced the Tilku (reincarnate Lama) system, and Gelug sect introduced Dalai Lama, and Panchen Lama system into their group.

In this late Vajrayana school of thought, Vairocana's primeval Buddha status has been replaced by other Buddhas such as Vajrasattva, Vajradhara, and Samanthabadra. Also there's the introduction of Yab-yum which symbolically represents the union of sexual polarity. What Yab-yum represents is one of the great symbolic mysticism of Vajrayana Buddhism, and it's true meaning is designed to be understood only by advanced student of its practice.

Loss of path to Nirvana

A detailed construction plan is needed to construct even a building. Then arguably, something that requires ultimate sophistication such as attaining Nirvana will need even more detailed blueprint to attain it. But beyond certain level, detailed plans to get there is missing from the scriptures.

There is no contiguous path set forth in the scriptures that will take disciples from a novice all the way to Nirvana. In a way, all of Mahayana, and Vajrayana Buddhism's effort was to resupply this missing knowledge that existed during Buddha's time. But it is almost certain that no one in the past 1000 years have attained Nirvana using these methods.

Theravada Buddhism is not fairing much better. Because knowledge of how to navigate one self in the etherial ream is missing from their scriptures as well. So it is impossible for the follower of Theravada Buddhism to make progress in this area.

Buddha states in Samyutta Nikaya (SN 51.13):

"When the four bases of spiritual power have been developed and cultivated in this way, a bhikkhu (monk) wields the various kinds of spiritual power: having been one, he becomes many; having been many, he becomes one; he appears and vanishes; he goes unhindered through a wall, through a rampart, through a mountain as though through space; he dives in and out of the earth as though it were water; he walks on water without sinking as though it were earth; seated cross-legged, he travels in space like a bird; with his hands he touches and strokes the moon and sun so powerful and mighty; he exercises mastery with the body as far as the brahmā world."

As seen in this statement, through Buddhist practices, monks were expected to gain siddhi, or super human powers as natural course of progress. Nirvana is a state existing outside of this universe. This would mean that one would need to cultivate the power to navigate themselves through this realm. But any discussion pertaining to the exact method for cultivating these powers cannot be found in the scriptures. The statement above says "When the four basis of spiritual power have been cultivated...". Four basis of spiritual power is commonly understood either as four concentration mentioned in the Bodhipakkyadhamma, namely:

Concentration (samadhi) of Five faculties (indriya), and Five powers (bala), Seven Factors of Enlightenment (bojjhanga), and Right Concentration of the Noble Eightfold Path.

or

iddipada (Four Basis of Power), namely concentration on:

1. Intention or purpose or desire or zeal (chanda)
2. Effort or energy or will (viriya)
3. Consciousness or mind or thoughts (citta)
4. Investigation or discrimination (*vimamsa)*

So there are descriptions about some of the ways to attain these powers, but no detailed methods are given in the scriptures. Buddha himself states the importance of development of these powers as:

"Bhikkhus, those who have neglected the four bases for spiritual power have neglected the noble path leading to the complete destruction of suffering. Those who have undertaken the four bases for spiritual power have undertaken the noble path leading to the destruction of suffering." (Samyutta Nikaya 51.2)

For something so important, shouldn't there be a description on how to practice them ?

In India, there is a religious tradition called Guru-Sheesha (Master to student) relationship. This indicates a private relationship between each student to their teacher. It is conceivable that these knowledge were passed on to the student when the student was ready to practice them, but were not part of the general discourse. Since they were not openly discussed, they never entered the scriptures.

In the days of the Buddha, Buddha himself would fill in any missing informations. Student today wouldn't have this luxury because in this world there's no teacher who can guide a student in this area.

Some exceptionally talented students may have succeeded in the past. There are people in Zen community, and Vajrayana Buddhism who were, and are able to demonstrate siddhi or supernatural powers throughout the ages. Some may have found their way into Nirvana by their own practice, but an integrated way of how to achieve it has not been written down into a text.

Therefore the path to Nirvana that existed during the time of the Buddha may be said to be lost at this point.

In fact, this problem has become so insurmountable, that I see general attitude of giving up the endeavor even amongst the professional monks.

What are missing from the scriptures ?

Since there are no mentions made about informations left out on how to attain these powers in the scriptures, we can only deduce them by comparing what's written in the agamas (scriptures based on Buddha's words) about the powers monks in Buddha's time were attaining, and teachings not found in the agamas in regards to how to attain them. When we go through this subtractive process, we see informations are lacking in the following areas:

1. Methods for attaining power (Siddhi)

2. Meditative and/or astral/physiological techniques used to attain them

3. If the practice requires any external assistance

4. How these powers gained should be used to attain enlightenment

5. What dangers (if there are any) we should be aware of before embarking on these practices

Number five in the list is especially noteworthy. If these informations were intentionally omitted from the scriptures, there must be a reason for it. It would be criminally negligent to put informations that may harm a practitioner into the scriptures without some warning. But even if warnings were heeded, some may attempt the practice, and harm themselves. In such cases, the only guaranteed safe way would be to leave the information out altogether. If this be the case, then there are:

Changes that takes place deep within one self that is not controllable by normal means when one performs these practices.

Then it requires supervision by a more senior monk to guide the novice through the process. We also don't know why these powers are important in attaining enlightenment, and instructions about their usages are necessary. In short, we need a teacher to guide us through these developmental processes.

The teacher in this case needs to have skill, and power to guide the student. The only ones truly qualified in this fashion are the Buddhas themselves. In fact there is no other way of attaining Nirvana without their guidance. This issue will be further discussed, and addressed in the following chapters of this book.

Was it meant to end this way ?

Buddha said Buddhism will survive for 500 years after his entry into Nirvana. It's been 2500 years since Buddha entered nirvana. If Buddha's word was correct, it would have been futile to attempt to attain Nirvana beyond the 500th year after his parinibbhana.

Was Buddhism which is one of crowning achievement of humanity, and spirituality destined to perish after such short amount of time ? Fortunately for us, Buddha have thought about, and devised a way to attain Nirvana even in this modern age. We will look into the methods we are left with in the following chapters.

A path that was prepared by the Buddha

There are many wondrous things Buddha has done during his days on earth. His teachings went even to those who live in the heavens. He was able to see into the past, and future with equal ease. Would such person not be capable of setting gateways for future seekers of liberation ?

In fact, that is exactly what he has done, and a well thought out path has been prepared for future generations.

Following sections of this book is dedicated to this path which was prepared by the Buddha. It is a very streamlined path that any of us with interest can partake, and also powerful enough to allow entry into Nirvana.

In a way, we are fortunate to be living in this time which is relatively short time in Buddhist scale after the Buddha's appearance. We are still in the time where scriptures are in good condition, and easily accessible thanks to the modern information technology. If we were born before the Buddha's time, there would have been no chance to learn his teachings, and if we weren't born in the time when information wasn't so readily available, we would have had much more difficult time finding our way.

So we should consider ourselves fortunate, and move forward in our path.

Sometimes the best things are hidden in the simplest of things.

Part 2:

The Practice

Chundi Buddha Mother

Pantheon of Buddhas, and Chundi Buddha

During the course of Vajrayana Buddhism's development, mandala, and along with it pantheon of Buddhas appeared. Each Buddha in this pantheon represents unique power that benefits the practitioner. One of the Buddha in this pantheon is Chundi (sometimes spelled Cundi). Chundi is important in that her function is to aid humans in entering the path to Buddhahood. Chundi means "Pure", and she is also known as Saptakoṭibuddhamātṛ, or mother of 70 million Buddhas. As her name suggests, she is a mother of future Buddhas. Chundi is unique in that she develops both monks, and householders in their Buddhistic practices. Especially for householders, she is known to guide one's path in Buddhism even if they are married, drink's alcoholic beverages, and engages in worldly affairs.

One may wonder why a pantheon of Buddhas appeared in Buddhism even though Buddha Shakyamuni never mentioned about its existence. This is because all the Buddhas in this pantheon except for Buddha Shakyamuni, Amogasiddhi, Virocana (The Sun Buddha), and some of the Adi (primeval) Buddhas were all Buddha Shakyamuni's disciples who've attained enlightenment under him. So this pantheon didn't exist when he first started his teachings.

It seems that this fact was known to some Buddhist monks who had the power to perceive into the spiritual realm. Following stanza which is attributed to Nagarjuna - who is one of the founders of the Madhyamaka school of Buddhism, states the benefit of seeking refuge in Chundi in the following way:

" If one chants Chundi's mantra everyday with tranquil heart, one will escape harm even if one experiences accident or calamity. Gods, and human will experience blessings equal to those of the Buddha. If practice is done under this all granting jewel, one will attain Buddha's equanimity (enlightenment). If my prayer isn't realized, I will accept the punishment of not being able to enter Nirvana myself."

It seems from this statement, Nagarjuna was aware of Buddha Mother's spiritual assistance long before Vajrayana Buddhism came about.

By the 4th century she was commonly known, and Maha Cundi Dharani sutra was written around this time. By the 7th century, first translation of this sutra into Chinese was done by Subhakrasimha (637 - 735 CE) . Two other translation followed, done by Vajrabodhi (669 - 741 CE), and Amoghavajra (705 - 774 CE).

Why is Chundi the Buddha to take refuge under ?

It is common in Vajrayana Buddhism for a practitioner to invite a Buddha into their practice. Many practice exists in Vajrayana Buddhism with specific Buddha or a deity at the center of its practice. In Shingon sect of Vajrayana Buddhism, Chundi is recognized as the Buddha that offers guidance to the human world. Furthermore, through her own commitment, Chundi took on the responsibility to offer her guidance to humanity.

This is why Chundi is the Buddha to take refuge under. In Vajrayana Buddhism, she is the only one who helps both laymen, and monks. And as a Vajrayana tradition, Buddha who helps the practitioner is invited into the practice by recitation of their mantra. So even in laymen's case, her mantra is chanted, and her mudra is formed to access her powers.

Who is Chundi ?

Since not much has been written about Chundi in the scriptures, there are many speculations about who, or what she is. Some say she is another incarnation of Durga - an Indian deity, or Chandi who's another Indian deity. She is also believed to be a Quan-in or a bodhisattva, because her appearance expressed in many arts, and sculptures closely resembles that of Avalokitashuvara. There's also a belief that she is an alter-ego of Buddha Bhaiṣajya-guru. Others say she's formed directly from part of Virocana, and was pure from the start. All of these are false. She was a living person who was an ordained nun (bhikkhuni) at the time of Buddha Shakyamuni.

She has attained Buddhahood during the time of Buddha Shakyamuni, and is often represented with the appearance like that of Avalokitashuvara. In Chundi Dharani Sutra she is said to have three eyes, and 18 arms. Other sources has variations in the number of her arms from 2 to 84. Each of the arms hold instrument that helps the practitioner.

Artist's rendition of Chundi Buddha Mother

The eighteen arms of Chundi are said to express the eighteen merits of attaining Buddhahood. These are the eighteen uncommon qualities. Her arms are the symbolic expression of these secrets, endowed with the significance of profound principles. In the Mahaprajnaparamita-sastra, these eighteen characteristics of a buddha (the avenikadharma) distinguish a buddha from a bodhisattva. They are:

1. His perfection of body
2. His perfection of speech
3. His perfection of memory
4. His perfection of impartiality to all
5. His serenity
6. His self-sacrifice
7. His unceasing desire to salvage sentient beings
8. His unflagging zeal to salvage sentient beings
9. His unfailing thought to salvage sentient beings
10. The unceasing wisdom to salvage sentient beings
11. The powers of deliverance
12. The principle of the powers of deliverance
13. Revealing perfect wisdom in deed
14. Revealing perfect wisdom in word
15. Revealing perfect wisdom in thought
16. Perfect knowledge of the past
17. Perfect knowledge of the future
18. Perfect knowledge of the present

Chundi was not well known in the west because Vajrayana Buddhism itself was not well known throughout the world. It's teachings were traditionally hidden in secrecy, and it is only in the recent 30 - 40 years that Vajrayana Buddhism began to have its presence known. Vajrayana Buddhism is called secret teachings in Japan, and as the name implies, it's teachings were not to be disclosed to the public. But there are now few Vajrayana Buddhism based sect that teaches to the public. This book is one of the first to bring informations about Chundi to the world.

Chundi as the Buddha Mother

Chundi has two main aspects to her work in the human world. One is to provide protection, and another to provide guidance in Buddhist studies to both householders, and monks. Chundi is one of the few Buddha that a relationship can be formed relatively easily, even by those who are not versed in Buddhist practices.

As the name Buddha Mother implies, Chundi aids in developing individuals in Buddhist practice. Chundi provides protection in various area of one's life as well. In this sense, Chundi's effect on one's life is not just in spiritual areas. There will be subtle but qualitative improvement in many area of one's life. Practitioners also receives protection from various calamities. There will be spiritual peace in their life. Order will be restored in one's life, and it becomes easier to conduct one's daily activities.

There will be significant improvement in monk's practice also. One of the issues mentioned earlier was difficulty of understanding Buddha's method for reaching Nirvana. When one develops relationship with Chundi, missing informations from the scriptures will be imparted directly by her when the disciple is ready. Chundi will also aid the disciples with their meditation. In this way, difficult areas of Buddhist practice will be made considerably easier.

* * * *

Perhaps the most important step for a Buddhist is to become a Steam Winner (Sotāpanna). This is because once one's a stream winner, they are guaranteed to attain Nirvana. A Stream Winner will attain enlightenment within maximum of next seven human incarnations. During these reincarnation, one is always reborn as a human being or in a heavenly realm, and never reincarnates into a lower form of existence. In order to attain Stream Winner status, practitioner must eradicate what Buddhist calls the "Three lower fetters". The three lower fetters are:

1. **Self-view** - The speculative view that a so-called *self* exists in the five aggregates (physical forms, feelings/sensations, perception, mental formations and consciousness) is eradicated because the Sotāpanna gains insight into the selfless nature of the aggregates.
2. **Skeptical Doubt** - Doubt about the Buddha and his teaching is eradicated because the Sotāpanna personally experiences the true nature of reality through insight, and this insight confirms the accuracy of the Buddha's teaching.
3. **Clinging to rites and rituals** - Clinging to the view that one becomes pure simply through performing ritual or rigid moralism, such as relying in a god for non-causal deliverance, slaughtering animals for sacrifice, ablutions, etc. is eradicated because the Sotāpanna realizes that the excessive rites and ritual are nothing more than an obstructive tradition.

By performing Buddha Mother's practice daily, one develops the understanding that;

1. A divine being exists in this universe,
2. That their moral conduct is perfect,
3. That they have unlimited power,
4. That they are interested in the well being of the individual, the society, the country, and the world,

This helps to remove skeptical doubt about Buddha's teachings, and one is aided in losing one of the lower fetters.

By cultivating relationship with Chundi, one can ask for advise, ask for spiritual protection, ask for material protection, and ask for removal of one's negative karma.

In this way, Chundi Buddha Mother aids the student of Buddhism, in entering the path to Nirvana.

Removal of one's negative Karma

Removal of one's negative karma is one of the central theme for any spiritual aspirant. But there are two limitations that makes this difficult:

One is how would an individual detect their own karma ?
Other is once detected, how would the individual remove the karma ?

Both abilities are normally beyond the reach of a practitioner. But through one's daily practice, Buddha Mother will remove one's negative karma gradually.

Negative karma are not turned "on" all the time, but bears fruit when conditions becomes ripe. This can be understood by a small example of if a person had the karma to be bitten by a snake, that karma cannot bear fruit where there are no snakes. In order for the karmic seed to germinate, it needs to have the proper condition. This means that karma will not bear fruit randomly, but it seeks it's own fruition ground. But by performing the Chundi mantra on a daily basis, it will have the effect of greatly attenuating one's negative karmic influence - sometimes eradicating them completely.

For instance, lets take an example of what happened to a certain individual.

One day he had a head on collision with another car with both cars going at substantial speed. He walked away from it unscathed. He never even had to go to the hospital. His car was totaled, and the insurance inspector who came to check the car out said, "The person in this car is dead.". The inspector has seen many cars that had accident in his career, and a car with that much damage was always fatal to the driver. This individual recounted the incident saying "If I wasn't working on my practice (that involved chanting Chundi mantra every day), I probably would have been dead when that accident happened.".

In his case, effect of his past karma took place, but it did not bear fruit of his death.

In this way, there will often be notable incident that indicates to the practitioner that their negative karma has taken effect, but they often walk away from them feeling "How did I get out of that ?".

Another area where one's negative karma might show up is in choosing one's partner in life. In the movie "Pretty Woman", the character played by Julia Roberts says "My mom says I'm a bum magnet.". This is a very insightful statement. What makes us attracted to one type of an individual and not the other ? If the negative pattern repeats itself in one's life as Julia Roberts' character says, one can suspect that a karmic effect is taking place. We make hundreds if not thousands of decisions everyday. Karma often manifest itself in key decisions we make without us even knowing about it. It is indeed difficult for us to deprogram ourselves from making the wrong decision that leads us to our own down fall, because these subconscious programming are nearly impossible to detect by ourselves. By performing practice indicated in this book on a daily basis, these undesirable characteristics will gradually disappear, and positive results starts to appear.

The Practice

Who this practice is for

The practice can be performed by both laymen and monks. In it's simplest form, it takes less than five minutes each day to perform this practice. This is a Buddhist practice, but it is not necessary to join any particular Buddhist organization. This is because the relation is formed directly between the practitioner, and Chundi Buddha Mother.

How to perform the Practice

Following is the practice:

One should be appropriately dressed in a respectable clothing.

First prostrate to Chundi, and all the Buddhas by chanting the following mantra.

> Om sarva tathagata pada-vandanam karomi
> (I prostrate at the feet of all the Buddhas/Tathagatas)

Then recite the following Chundi mantra thirty times with Chundi mudra (see picture below) held at your chest level.

NAMO SAPTANAM SAMYAKSAMBUDDHA KOTINAM.
TADYATHA: OM! CALE, CULE, CHUNDI SVAHA!

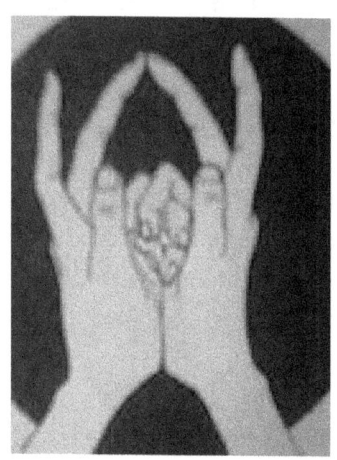

Recite Shakyamuni Buddha's mantra once.

Oṃ muni muni mahāmuni śākyamuni svāhā

Prostrate again with the mantra.

Om sarva tathagata pada-vandanam karomi

This is all it takes.

The practice can be accompanied by offering of incense, and water to Chundi Buddha Mother, and the Buddhas.

The practice should be performed once a day, but this doesn't mean that it must be done before midnight. It can be performed up to the time you go to sleep.

Building relationship with Chundi Buddha Mother, and the Buddhas

The practice is cumulative, and relation with Buddha Mother becomes stronger over time. Although Chundi Buddha Mother will come to you from the first day of practice, it takes about 600 days of daily practice before one can feel the build up of Buddha Mother's power within oneself. If one's practice pattern is irregular, effect of the practice will also be so.

600 days may seem long, but this is little more than year and a half's time, and it will pass rather quickly. The difficult part is doing it once a day, and continue the practice for 600 days strait.

How long should the practice be performed ?

The practice needs to performed throughout one's life. Once one stops performing the practice, relationship with Buddha Mother wanes, and eventually disappears. So, proper maintenance of this relationship must be done in order to keep one self in the path.

Practice for the monks

The first part of the practice for monks is the same as that of the the householders. Monks need's to recite Chundi mantra, accompanied by Buddha Shakyamuni's mantra. The difference is, for monks, more they recite Chundi mantra. better effect it will have on their development.

Second part of the practice for monks entail a special meditation that involves inviting Chundi to their meditation. Inviting a Buddha into one's meditation is the critical part of Buddha's practice that was left out of scriptures. This is because it is pure exercise in meditation which doesn't require explanation. In this meditation, Chundi will directly inject her power into the practitioner's body. This has two separate effect on the practitioner's body. First is the gradual transformation of their spiritual body into that of the Buddha's. Second is the injection of Buddha's power into their body. Chundi's power is very strong, and the energy that is imparted is greater than what a normal human body can generate on its own.

It is also highly recommended that the practicing monk take on some sort of human energy field training such as chi-kung before embarking on this meditation. This is so that they can observe the effect of this power more readily, and understand its nature.

The second part of the practice goes as follows:

Set aside a block of time such as 30 minutes, one hour etc. Make sure that you wouldn't need to go anywhere during this time. Interruption is not only detrimental, but may be harmful to the practitioner.

Sit in a meditative posture. Relax and recite the following:

"Chundi, please come in to my meditation, and impart your sequence of energy exercise to my being. I submit to your grace, and compassion for giving me this energy."

Then resume your meditation, keeping calm, focused, and still.

After the meditation is over, prostrate to the Buddha, and the practice is over.

The effect of this practice is cumulative. More power builds up longer the practice is performed.

It is not certain when one starts to manifest siddhi. But one can expect to be on this practice for ten years or longer before these powers starts to manifest. But long before this happens, one should be able to tell the magnitude of power that is being infused into one's body. The awareness of the existence of this power in one's body should convince them that special change is happening to them.

Keeping celibacy is an important aspect of this practice. Energy gained in this meditation will be lost, and destabilization of the energy may occur if celibacy is not maintained. For this reason, you must be sure that you can maintain celibacy while you are performing this practice. As a monk, celibacy is expected as part of their monastic practice. Part of the reason why Buddha's disciples were expected to be celibate is also from this reason.

The practice must be done in conjunction with Chundi mantra practice so the practitioner can obtain instructions regarding other parts of the practice from Chundi.

Third part of monk's practice is to adhere to the vinayas (laws monks must follow). Buddha's rules for monks were designed to attenuate the effect of dependent origins until they eventually come to a stop.

Buddha's methods are multi-faceted. One aspect is to slow down the effect of dependent origins, the other is to gain enough power to freely move in other dimensions. Still other is to gain control of one's own mind, and consciousness. Yet another is to prevent new karma from rising. All of these comprise the Buddha's method.

So monks should put all of these available methods into practice, and as Buddha has always said, observe carefully what is happening to oneself.

Monks may also request Buddha Mother to assist them with their meditation, and various questions that may arise during their practice. This channel for forming personal relationship with an active Buddha is the unique feature of this practice.

Areas of knowledge that are difficult to understand can be gained directly from Buddha Mother's transmissions.

We've discussed about the loss of path to Nirvana in the previous chapters. Mystery was why was Buddha's disciples were able to master what seems impossibly difficult powers in relatively short time. The incredible powers they've gained to transcend the world is out of reach by ordinary human means. This was because Buddha himself was imparting his power to the disciples, and these results which leads to enlightenment are unattainable by normal human efforts.

Chundi Buddha Mother will transmit the power needed to accomplish the same meditation Buddha Shakyamuni's disciples were practicing to augment Buddhist practices of today. The method does not conflict any school of Buddhism, but rather works to compliment it. This is because good meditation practice is at the core of every Buddhist sects.

This method has been lost for ages. Now the method is restored, and the path to Nirvana is open again. Buddhas has never stopped sending their support to our world. It only takes the effort on our part to take advantage of it.

Studying the Buddhist scriptures

During the course of the practice, it is recommended that some Buddhist scriptures be read, and studied. These includes Therabada, yogacara, and Vajrayana scriptures.

This is because it is much quicker and easier to learn from reading the scriptures. If one has access to the scriptures, it is recommended that they read them as much as possible.

But even for those who don't have access to the scriptures, Buddha Mother can provide knowledge through experience, as to how one can progress in the practice.

When will I start seeing the results ?

Chundi Buddha Mother's protection starts immediately as the practice starts, but one will feel the presence of Chundi more as the relation builds up. It takes about 5 - 600 days for the relationship grows to its full strength. There should be increase of peace in one's life, and life starts to get better organized, which seems to be the general side effect of being associated with the Buddhas. These along with the purification, and protection mentioned earlier will start to take place as practice progresses.

To obtain blessings of other Seven Protector Buddhas, one need's to recite their mantra once a day as part of the daily practice. The synergistic effect will show up after a period of time.

What to do when the effect does not take place ?

Sometimes the practice doesn't take effect, or effect wanes during one's practice. This is always due to one violating one of Buddhists moral precepts.

For laymen, and monks, the rules are different. Monks must follow the oath of the monks. Laymen need's to adhere to their moral codes of conduct which is mentioned in the following section.

Keeping Moral Precepts

It is recommended that for effects of the aforementioned practices to take place, householders abstain from amoral behaviors. This includes the following five precepts, and abstinence from the sixteen defilements of the mind.

The Five Precepts:

1. Abstinence from taking life.
2. Abstinence from taking what is not given.
3. Abstinence of sexual misconduct.
4. Abstinence from false speech.
5. Abstinence from taking fermented drink that causes heedlessness.

The Sixteen Defilements of Mind:

1. abhijjha-visama-lobha, covetousness and unrighteous greed
2. byapada, ill will
3. kodha, anger
4. upanaha, hostility or malice
5. makkha, denigration or detraction; contempt
6. palasa, domineering or presumption
7. issa, envy

8. *macchariya,* jealousy, or avarice; selfishness
9. *maya,* hypocrisy or deceit
10. *satheyya,* fraud
11. *thambha,* obstinacy, obduracy
12. *sarambha,* presumption or rivalry; impetuosity
13. *mana,* conceit
14. *atimana,* arrogance, haughtiness
15. *mada,* vanity or pride
16. *pamada,* negligence or heedlessness; in social behavior, this leads to lack of consideration.

When problem persists

When things aren't going well in one's life even after the aforementioned moral precepts are kept, they should consider if one of the following may be affecting their life:

1. Affliction due to spiritual cause
2. Afflictions due to one's own karma

There are more problems caused in one's life than one may realize from spiritual causes. In the age when material science is considered supreme, talking about ghosts and spirits usually draws ridicules. But in Buddhism, existence of spiritual entities are acknowledged as part of the construct of this world. The issue is that most practitioners do not posses detection capability of these spiritual entities. But if one suspects that something is not of the "norm", they may request Buddha Mother to remove these suspected spiritual afflictions. In some case the cause is not due to a single spiritual affliction, but entails multiple spiritual afflictions. Then request should be repeated until all suspected spiritual afflictions are removed. As one becomes skilled in this area, their sensitivity to spiritual entities increases, and becomes easier to detect them. Spiritual afflictions can also be from living entities. Other people's intent has effect on our person, and if this is suspected, a request can be made to Buddha Mother for protection, and their removal.

Karmic afflictions often are easier to detect because they often shows up in our daily lives. The earlier example of Julia Roberts' character in the movie "Pretty Woman" always attracting certain types of men to her is an example of karma in action. If certain pattern that is out side of one's intention appears repeatedly, one can almost be certain that it is due to karma in action.

In both cases, practitioner can request assistance from Buddha Mother to remove the spiritual affliction, or karmic affliction. One should be open to be shown their own issues if the cause of negativity lies in one's own acts. Otherwise the undesirable behavior will continue, and their karmic effect cannot be stopped.

There's also sometimes an issue of bogus problems in one's life where it's from their ego's perspective that something is not going right. In this case things are fine, but perception is that it is not. It's simple to say that one's deluded in this case, but this is a very difficult mistake to get out of. If Buddha Mother's suggestion consistently conflict with one's perception, it's worthwhile to investigate that something one's not aware of, or situation never considered is what is actually happening.

These are somewhat advanced topics, and one should not expect to have immediate mastery of situations described above. They are presented here as something to be aware of for future studies. These techniques requires much experience before one can discern the true cause of the problem. Through experiencing problems, one becomes experienced, and becomes better at detecting their cause.

Chundi's fierce form

Most Buddha has an alter ego that is the exact opposite of their peaceful countenance. This is their fierce form, and their appearances are usually demonic looking. This is not because they have a violent side, but they take on these forms to educate those who are uneducable by other means. When a practitioner is so deluded that merely talking to them in a reasonable way can't bring them back into the path, Buddha sends its fierce form to frighten the individual back into the straight path.

Chundi's fierce form is called Ucchusma, and has a raging hair of fire, and is usually depicted with one leg lifted up ready to crush the disciple's ignorance. Ucchusma may manifest in a disciple's life in the form various difficulties, to make the individual understand that something is wrong in the way they're conducting their life.

Ucchusma

How to live as a Buddhist

Living as Buddhist has different requirements for laymen, and monks. Here how to live as Buddhist for laymen will be discussed. Monks have well defined rules they need to live by, and those rules should be observed. Monks should also follow the "Practice for Monks" explained earlier to reduce karma, gain astral development, and energy of the Buddha.

Taking on the practice

The practice involving recitation of the Chundi mantra explained earlier should be practiced on a daily basis. Benefit of this practice is significant in that it entails reduction of one's karma, and development of their spiritual bodies. Continuation of this practice moves the practitioner towards becoming a Stream Winner.

Living a moral life

As mentioned in the previous chapter, keeping moral precepts is an important part of Buddhist life. List of precepts to keep, and defilements that one should stay away from is listed here again for reference. People commit evil deeds thinking "It's such a small thing, it wouldn't make much difference.". But these small deeds accumulate to produce large results, so one's moral precepts must be guarded carefully.

The Five Precepts:

1. Abstinence from taking life.
2. Abstinence from taking what is not given.
3. Abstinence of sexual misconduct.
4. Abstinence from false speech.
5. Abstinence from taking fermented drink that causes heedlessness.

The Sixteen Defilements of Mind:

1. abhijjha-visama-lobha, covetousness and unrighteous greed
2. byapada, ill will
3. kodha, anger
4. upanaha, hostility or malice
5. makkha, denigration or detraction; contempt
6. palasa, domineering or presumption
7. issa, envy
8. macchariya, jealousy, or avarice; selfishness
9. maya, hypocrisy or deceit
10. satheyya, fraud
11. thambha, obstinacy, obduracy
12. sarambha, presumption or rivalry; impetuosity
13. mana, conceit
14. atimana, arrogance, haughtiness
15. mada, vanity or pride

16. pamada, negligence or heedlessness; in social behavior, this leads to lack of consideration.

Doing good

Doing good is also an important component of Buddhist life. Good deeds not only benefit the individual who performs them, but has wide reaching effect on both the society, and the environment. Good deeds also becomes a deterrent to bad things from happening to the individual's life. Buddha explains why this is so in the following agama:

"It is as if, O priests, a man were to put a lump of salt into a small cup of water. What think ye, O priests? Would now the small amount of water in this cup be made salt and undrinkable by the lump of salt?"

"Yes, Reverend Sir."

"And why?"

"Because, Reverend Sir, there was but a small amount of water in the cup, and so it was made salt and undrinkable by the lump of salt."

"It is as if, O priests, a man were to throw a lump of salt into the river Ganges. What think ye, O priests? Would now the river Ganges be made salt and undrinkable by the lump of salt?"

"Nay, verily, Reverend Sir."

"And why not?"

"Because, Reverend Sir, the mass of water in the river Ganges is great, and so is not made salt and undrinkable by the lump of salt."

"In exactly the same way, O priests, we may have the case of an individual who does some slight deed of wickedness which brings him to hell; or, again, O priests, we may have the case of another individual who does the same slight deed of wickedness, and expiates it in the present life, though it may be in a way which appears to him not slight but grievous.

(Anguttara-Nikâya (iii.33))

Here Buddha explains that the fruit of one's action depends on the balance of good and evil deeds one has performed. If one has performed much good deeds that helped others, and the world around them, it becomes one's merit which protects them from being in the harms way. Often people dismiss doing good thinking "It's such a small thing, it won't make much difference whether I do it or not.". But this is not true, as the effect of doing good are also accumulative. So good deeds has good effect all around for both the ones that receives them, and the individual who performs them.

Building merit

As mentioned above, meritorious actions not only benefits the environment, but helps to protect the individual as well. It is believed in Buddhism that even a meal one eats is a product of one's own past merit. In this sense, even simple acts should not be taken lightly.

Many wonder why people are born into different conditions. In Buddhism, this is attributed to their past karma. Past karma can be changed by present effort. This is also the reason why religious practice is worth taking. This is also an invitation that if there's an area of one's life where one is not satisfied with, efforts can be made to change their conditions.

The Seven Protector Buddhas of the World

Although Buddha's powers are limitless, Buddhas in Vajrayana pantheon has specialties in their areas of power. Buddha Mother works with six other Buddhas when it comes to matters regarding the world. For issues outside of one's normal practice that involves the world, requests can be made to these Buddhas for the betterment of its condition.

The seven Buddhas of world protection

There are Buddhas that are closely related to Chundi that brings protection, and welfare to the world. These Buddhas works with Chundi in matters that requires their specialties. One can make requests regarding the world to these Buddhas for its protection.

There are matters of this world that are beyond the scope of a normal human being. But often a situation requires for a corrective action. In these cases, a request may be made to the Buddha Mother, and other Buddhas that she works with. These issues may be of material nature, or they can be of spiritual nature.

Human world belongs to the humans, and Buddhas of the Buddha realm will not intercede with the workings of the human world unless us humans specifically asks for them. The proper maintenance of our world is our responsibility, but by inviting these Buddhas to work with us, they can use their powers to help situations of our world.

There are total of seven Buddhas who works in this capacity including Chundi Buddha Mother. The names and the characters of these Buddhas are presented in the following section.

The Buddhas presented here can assist the practitioner with their practice as well, asides from offering protection to the world.

Characteristics of the Seven Protector Buddhas

Chundi

She is the Buddha of educating, and guiding disciples in the modern world. She is accessible to both laymen, and monks which makes her the ideal guru to seek refuge under.

Shakyamuni

Shakyamuni is the original Buddha that started Buddhism. He's also the one who passed his torch to Chundi after they attained liberation. For this reason, his mantra is recited along with Chundi's in the daily practice.

Amitaba

Amitaba has been focus of worship amongst the laymen, and monks throughout history. What is not well known about Amitaba is the he is the masculine alter ego of Chundi.

Buddhas have the ability to split their bodies into different identities. So it is common for a Buddha to have multiple identities.

With Amitaba being the alter ego of Chundi, it is not surprising that their functions are also similar. That is to be accessible to the laypeople of this world.

The chief difference between the two is in that Chundi is a Vajrayana Buddha, and as such has strong function as a teacher, whereas Amitaba is both Mahayana, and Vajrayana Buddha, and offers path of salvation to the uneducated masses. The intricate teachings of Buddha were out of reach for most people throughout the ages. Amitaba's pure land offers a training ground conducive to further development of Buddha qualities of the individual where an individual can advance in conditions more conducive to their Buddhist studies.

Amitaba is also Buddha of the Five Dhayani Buddahs of Vajrayana Buddhism, and represents light, and wisdom of discrimination.

Amoghasiddhi

Amoghasiddhi is also one of the Five Dhayani Buddahs of Vajrayana Buddhism. What is not commonly known about Amoghasiddhi is that he is an alter ego of Buddha Shakyamuni. The name means "He whose accomplishment won't end vainly (won't be without result)". Which is interesting when one considers "Siddhartha", the birth name of Buddha Shakyamuni also meant "One who attained the goal ".

Amoghasiddhi is the Buddha of all accomplishing wisdom. He is venerated for his power to attain success. Amoghasiddhi also imparts courage to take on, and accomplish the necessary task.

Ability to complete the task without failure is important in undertaking any task. Amoghasiddhi aids the practitioner to accomplish the tasks required to attain their Buddhahood.

Chintamani Chakra

Chintamani Chakra's name is comprised of words Chintamani which is a jewel that has power to grant one's wishes, and Chakra which means wheel, but in this case wheel of Buddhist

Dharma. In Tendai, and Shingon sects of Japan, she is regarded as the Quan-in in charge of the the godly realm. Since Chundi is the Buddha of the human world, and Chintamani Chakra is the Buddha of the heavenly realm, one can see the close relationship between the two Buddhas. The two are often regarded to work together to accomplish a common task. Chintamani Chakra supports the practitioner in the heavenly realm with their Buddhist practice. There the practitioner continues their Buddhist practice under more favorable condition for attaining Buddhahood.

Ratnasambhava

Ratnasambhava is one of the Five Dhayani Buddahs of Vajrayana Buddhism. Ratna in his name means "jem", and Ratnasambhava means jewel born. His mudra is dana or giving. All of this not surprisingly comes to mean Ratnasambhava as the Buddha that imparts wealth to the practitioner.

Akashagarba (or Vajra "Ratna") is his alter ego, and his wrathful manifestation is Kundali which makes for an interesting combination. Akashagarba is the Bodhisattva that is known to impart opening of sahasrara chakra to those who chant his mantra, and Kundali is believed to symbolize rising of kundalini, or the feminine force within one's body. The two symbolizes the merging of masculine, and feminine forces within one's body. So Ratnasambhava symbolizes the secrets of tantra or attainment of enlightenment through tantric methods.

Vairocana

Vairocana is one of the Five Dhayani Buddahs of Vajrayana Buddhism. He is the primeval Buddha or the Adi Buddha that started Buddhism. All Buddhas are supposed to be the same, but amongst their sameness, they are believed to display their particular core strength. This is symbolized in the characteristics of the four Dhayani Buddhas. Virocana which is the White Buddha, like color white is combination of the primary colors, contains all the characteristics of the other Buddhas.

Vairocane is eternally teaching Buddhism to other Buddhas, and Bodhisattvas. Some Bodhisattvas were created from fragments of Virocana to help practitioners of Buddhism. Asides from Buddha Shakyamuni himself (and his alter ego such as Amoghasiddhi), Virocana and Bodhisattvas created by Vairocana, are the only Buddhas in the Buddhist pantheon that were not once Shakyamuni Buddha's disciples.

Incorporating Seven Protector Buddha's mantra into daily practice

Because Chundi, and Shakyamuni Buddha's mantra is already in the daily practice, only other five Buddha's mantra needs to be recited. This is recommended, but is optional. If the mantra of other Buddhas are incorporated into one's practice, the practitioner may expect support from these Buddhas as well.

Amitaba Buddha's mantra

Oṃ amṛta-teje hara hūṃ

Amoghasiddhi Buddha's mantra

Oṃ Amoghasiddhi

Chintamani Chakra Buddha's mantra

Oṃ Chintamani Chakra

Ratnasambhava Buddha's mantra

Oṃ ra tna saṃ bha va traṃ

Vairocana Buddha's mantra

Om Vairocana hum

Making request to the Seven Protector Buddhas of the World

If one has concern about the world that goes beyond the daily practice, or confines of one's everyday life, a request may be made to the Seven Protector Buddhas to help aid the situation. Although Buddhas are beings with infinite power, they are not a resident of this world. As such they usually will not intervene in this world's affairs unless request is made by those who are residents of this world. But as a human being, one can intercede in behalf of this world, and make requests to them. These are beings of infinite wisdom, and powers to see future events, so destructive requests will not be honored. It is wise to consult the Buddha Mother before one makes the request to see if the request is appropriate for the world at the present time. To make the request, one only needs to say or write down the following with the blank area filled in with their request.

" O' Seven Protector Buddhas of the World, please help the world by _____. "

This innocuously simple request works to better the world. One should not believe that an effort by one small human being wouldn't change the world. If one truly believes that such request will benefit the world, these requests should be communicated to the Buddhas.

Postscript

Path to Nirvana

This is the first book in the west that introduce practitioner to Chundi's Buddhist practice.

The reason why this practice works is because of the power of Chundi Buddha Mother. She assists her students with their practice in the three critical areas of practice. These three areas are meditation, transmission of necessary knowledge, and ridding of negative karma.

This practice is the only way to attain spiritual development that makes possible the entry into Nirvana.

It is this author's wish that more people gains understanding of the power of Buddhism, and make progress towards their fruitful lives.

Bibliography

Historic Buddha Shakyamuni

http://buddhism.about.com/od/lifeofthebuddha/a/buddhalife.htm

The Life of Buddha - by A. Ferdinand Herold

http://www.sgilibrary.org/search_dict.php?id=2518

http://buddhasutra.com/files/first_teaching.htm

http://en.wikipedia.org/wiki/Jetavana

http://ja.wikipedia.org/wiki/涅槃経

Buddha's Teachings

http://en.wikipedia.org/wiki/Dukkha

http://ja.wikipedia.org/wiki/五蘊盛苦

http://en.wikipedia.org/wiki/Four_Noble_Truths

http://en.wikipedia.org/wiki/Bodhipakkhiyādhammā

http://mahajana.net/texts/kopia_lokalna/MANUAL07.html

http://en.wikipedia.org/wiki/Four_stages_of_enlightenment

http://en.wikipedia.org/wiki/Fetter_(Buddhism)

http://mahajana.net/texts/kopia_lokalna/MANUAL07.html

Latter Buddhist Developments

http://en.wikipedia.org/wiki/Early_Buddhist_schools

http://www.buddhanet.net/e-learning/buddhism/lifebuddha/2_32lbud.htm

http://en.wikipedia.org/wiki/Second_Buddhist_council

http://en.wikipedia.org/wiki/Third_Buddhist_council

http://en.wikipedia.org/wiki/Fourth_Buddhist_council

Theravada Buddhism

http://en.wikipedia.org/wiki/Theravada

https://en.wikipedia.org/wiki/Sarvastivada

Mahayana Buddhism

http://ja.wikipedia.org/wiki/大乗仏教

http://en.wikipedia.org/wiki/Madhyamaka

http://en.wikipedia.org/wiki/Yogacara

http://ja.wikipedia.org/wiki/法相宗

http://en.wikipedia.org/wiki/Eight_Consciousnesses

http://ja.wikipedia.org/wiki/阿頼耶識

Vajrayana Buddhism

http://en.wikipedia.org/wiki/Vajrayana

http://ja.wikipedia.org/wiki/法身普賢

http://en.wikipedia.org/wiki/Anuttarayoga_Tantra

Loss of Path to Nirvana

http://en.wikipedia.org/wiki/Iddhipada

Chundi Buddha Mother

http://ja.wikipedia.org/wiki/准胝観音

http://www.sakai.zaq.ne.jp/piicats/jyuntei1.htm

http://askville.amazon.com/Cundi-Bodhisattva/AnswerViewer.do?requestId=6825617

http://en.wikipedia.org/wiki/Cundi_(Buddhism)

http://bigocoro.blog53.fc2.com/blog-entry-1195.html

http://www.lapislazulitexts.com/articles/cundi_dharani

http://desktop2ch.tv/kyoto/1284094921/?ws=&v=rev

http://www.lapislazulitexts.com/cundi_dharani_sutra.html

http://en.wikipedia.org/wiki/Sotāpanna

The Practice

http://www.davidmoreton.com/echoes/ajikan.html

http://www.sakai.zaq.ne.jp/piicats/butsuinn.htm

http://www.sakai.zaq.ne.jp/piicats/jyuntei2.htm

http://www.visiblemantra.org/shakyamuni.html

When will I start seeing the Effect ?

http://en.wikipedia.org/wiki/Ucchusma

http://www.ususama.net/ususama.html

How to Live as a Buddhist

http://www.sacred-texts.com/bud/bits/bits040.htm

Seven Protector Buddhas of the World

http://en.wikipedia.org/wiki/Amitābha

http://en.wikipedia.org/wiki/Amoghasiddhi

http://ja.wikipedia.org/wiki/如意輪観音

http://en.wikipedia.org/wiki/Ratnasambhava

http://en.wikipedia.org/wiki/Vairocana

http://www.visiblemantra.org/amitabha.html

http://www.visiblemantra.org/vairocana.html

http://www.visiblemantra.org/ratnasambhava.html

http://ja.wikipedia.org/wiki/六観音
#.E5.85.AD.E8.A6.B3.E9.9F.B3

Cover

http://bigocoro.blog53.fc2.com/blog-entry-1195.html

http://buddhabe.tumblr.com/page/141

http://blogs.yahoo.co.jp/kubochannikki/29034388.html

http://www.tokubi.jp/company/detail.asp?id=39

http://www.tumblr.com/tagged/vairocana

http://www.namgyal.org/about/buddhism.cfm

http://www.artoflegendindia.com/cosmic-buddha-ratnasambhava-with-eight-p-28458.html

www.ingramcontent.com/pod-product-compliance
Lightning Source LLC
LaVergne TN
LVHW051842080426
835512LV00018B/3016